W9-AJS-971

# DIGITAL CAREER BUILDING™

## CAREER BUILDING THROUGH

# INTERACTIVE ONLINE GAMES

MEG SWAINE

ROSEN
PUBLISHING®

New York

Published in 2008 by The Rosen Publishing Group, Inc.
29 East 21st Street, New York, NY 10010

Copyright © 2008 by The Rosen Publishing Group, Inc.

First Edition

All rights reserved. No part of this book may be reproduced in any form without permission in writing from the publisher, except by a reviewer.

**Library of Congress Cataloging-in-Publication Data**

Swaine, Meg.
Career building through interactive online games / Meg Swaine. — 1st ed.
    p. cm. — (Digital career building)
Includes bibliographical references and index.
ISBN-13: 978-1-4042-1946-5
ISBN-10: 1-4042-1946-3
1. Electronic games industry—Vocational guidance. 2. Computer games—Programming—Vocational guidance. I. Title.
HD9993.E452S93 2007
794.8023—dc22

                                        2007001027


*Manufactured in the United States of America*

# CONTENTS

# CHAPTER ONE

# THE COMPUTER GAME INDUSTRY

In the past, video games were simple blocks or blips moving around a screen, like *PONG* or *Space Invaders*, and usually involved simple gameplay mechanics that were fun and easy to understand in a matter of minutes. But with the advent of home consoles and better sound and graphics, video games have become much more sophisticated.

Video games have come a long way in a short period of time, so the experiences of both the players and the developers have changed, even over just the past decade. In the beginning, video games were mainly played on arcade machines. *PONG* was the first at-home game, but the real fun started when Atari and Intellivision released

Professional football star Steve Heighway plays *PONG*, which was released in 1975 and was the first video game that could be played at home.

systems that allowed people to play their favorite games at home, including *Pac-Man* and *Space Invaders*. In the early 1980s, however, arcade machines were going out of style, and Atari's next home system, the 5200, didn't sell. To many people in the video game industry, this was known as "the crash." This was when Nintendo arrived on the scene and introduced the first NES console.

## Personal Computers Reinvigorate the Game Industry

At the same time as home video game systems were falling out of favor, the first user-friendly personal computers were being released, including the Apple II, TRS Color Computer, IBM's PC, and, most important, the Commodore 64. Not only did the C64 deliver great sound and graphics (for its time), it also featured an interface that allowed users to write their own simple games using the programming language BASIC. The manual offered beginner tips, and some magazines at the time printed line-by-line programs/games that could be typed up in BASIC and played. In a matter of minutes, a person could code a simple text exchange using a few basic commands.

The development of CD-ROM allowed games to be longer-playing, more elaborate, and more complex, since games could be run directly from the CD with little to install on the hard drive. Some of the major players of the industry began to emerge, such as Electronic Arts and Sony. Games were so much more complicated that rather than coding from scratch, the average player could use level editors for games like *Doom* or use

Home computer systems made it easier for game enthusiasts to experiment with programming code and learn how to make their own games.

Adventure Game Creator to create games that worked the same way as *Sam and Max* or *Maniac Mansion*.

Games today no longer just rely on quick hand-eye coordination. They are also more interactive stories that depend upon good decision-making and real-time simulations that require a range of tasks and skills. Video games have become a medium as entertaining and as lucrative as the film industry, while managing to be even more accessible to their audience. Through video games, anyone can stretch his or her creative muscles and love for gaming, with even the simplest of tools. A survey by the Entertainment Software Association (ESA) found that 61 percent of parents actually believe that games are a positive part of their children's lives.

## The Computer Game Business, Big and Small

Right now, more and more people have broadband Internet, and this is affecting the video game industry in a big way. For example, lots of people can simultaneously play massively multiplayer online role-playing games (MMORPGs) like *World of Warcraft* or *City of Heroes*. In addition, now smaller companies, or even individuals, can show off their game designing talents and deliver their games directly to the players, all on a small budget. Flash and game download sites are making it easier for people to access games without even leaving their computer chairs.

Yet there is still plenty of game business being generated by companies with huge development and marketing budgets. Major video game companies like

Electronic Arts and Nintendo are hiring people all the time to keep up with the demand of making new games. The companies that make the consoles—Microsoft, Nintendo, Sony—also license their code to companies that only make games. These game manufacturers are called third-party developers, and they hire all different types of talent—artists, designers, programmers, audio engineers, and game testers. Because the world of video games is such a young medium, every year there are new opportunities for people who are passionate about video games to contribute their talents.

And it's not just about PCs and consoles anymore. There's also a demand now to make games for mobile platforms—cell phones, PDAs, and handheld consoles. Mobile devices are a lot more sophisticated these days, enabling people to play games on them that are a little more complicated than the comparatively crude games of old, like *Snake!*

Video game sales last year added up to roughly $ 7 billion (according to the ESA). The genres that are making money are MMORPGs, real-time strategy games, sim (simulation) games, first-person shooters, *Grand Theft Auto* clones, sports games, and, of course, puzzle games.

**Gamasutra.com:** Gamasutra offers a wealth of info and news on the industry. It is also a great place for aspiring developers to connect with companies that are hiring. Registration is free, and you can post your résumé on its site. There are columns written by major industry professionals and reviews on the latest gaming-related books and software. Gamasutra is also associated with GameCareerGuide.com and *Game Developer* magazine, two useful sources for finding information about the best colleges for gamers and about breaking into the industry. Members can actively participate in the site by writing reviews or submitting work to one of the online galleries.

Gamasutra goes above and beyond a typical print magazine about video games by offering information in a variety of media. The Gamasutra podcast tackles a number of topics with industry professionals and features comprehensive coverage of major industry events, such as the Game Developers Conference. Sign up with Gamasutra for a customized electronic newsletter that provides you with weekly industry news and job postings. It's an easy way to remain current with the video game industry if you forget or are too busy to visit the Gamasutra Web site regularly.

## A Wide World of Games

While genres such as MMORPGs, sims, and strategy games account for the majority of sales and shelf space in the market, industry professionals are in constant discussion at conferences such as GDC (the Game Developers Conference) about where video games are going. Should games contain more story? Less story? What about games that educate? Should there be more focus on those? Are some games too violent? The industry is evolving day by day as seasoned industry professionals and new developers alike hash out what needs to be done to keep video games stimulating, popular, relevant, and cutting edge.

A lot of current titles are based on existing "properties," like the newest movies, books, or even other, older

The widely anticipated release of the movie *Star Wars Episode III: Revenge of the Sith* was preceded by its video game counterpart of the same name. This allowed fans to get a sneak peek into the plot and world of this high-budget flick.

games. For instance, you might have played Lego's *Star Wars II*, an amusing take on the original *Star Wars* trilogy, or maybe you picked up the latest *Nancy Drew* PC adventure. Film companies will often try to leverage a film's popularity by hiring a game development company to create a video game based on the film. More recently, other types of companies have even started to use video games to increase brand awareness. For instance, Burger King recently contracted a game company to create a series of games based around their royal "spokescharacter."

If you frequent Web sites like Newgrounds or Ebaum's World, you might be a fan of free Flash games that have been coded and uploaded by other people.

The Nintendo Wii is breaking new ground with handheld controllers that track a player's movements in real time. These new types of controllers make a game more interactive and, by extension, even more fun.

These are free, simple games that usually become popular via a type of marketing called viral marketing, which exploits the power of old-fashioned word of mouth through the latest technology—players e-mailing and texting their friends about their new favorite Flash game and forwarding links to the game site.

Other video games, like puzzle games or card games, are considered "casual games," the sort of games that appeal to a mass audience by being simple, with a lot of clever replay value. These games are starting to make up a considerable portion of the video game market.

Right now, new consoles, like the PS3 and the Wii, are being released. But the release of these new consoles

Handheld systems such as the PlayStation Portable (PSP) can now play games that have better graphics and more complicated gameplay. This means that more sophisticated console games can now be simultaneously released on handheld systems.

isn't just random; it is timed to accommodate new technology, like Blu-ray or HD (high definition). You also may have noticed that video game controllers are getting more sophisticated, too. The much acclaimed game *Guitar Hero* requires the use of a controller that looks like a small guitar. Nintendo's Wii has a controller that can follow players' movements, for games like *The Legend of Zelda: Twilight Princess*. As new technologies are developed, game companies have to keep an eye out for innovations that will enhance a player's experience and make video games even more fun than before.

As you can see, the world of video games has become broad and sophisticated. There has never been a better, more fertile time to enter the field and put your passion for games and your digital skills to work. All it takes is curiosity and drive to make games that you yourself would like to see on the shelves.

# CHAPTER TWO

# UPSTARTS WHO BECAME INDUSTRY STANDOUTS

The number of big-budget games placed on the shelves by companies like Microsoft or Electronic Arts might make you wonder if you could possibly make a big impression in the gaming world, even with just simple projects. How can you compete with these billion-dollar titans of the industry? But believe it or not, there have been some instances in which what started out as a low-budget labor of love ended up being a high-profile sensation.

## HomestarRunner

Perhaps nobody is as familiar with lasting digital fame as Mike and Matt Chapman (the "Brothers Chaps"),

Think you can't do better than Nintendo at making games? Give it a shot! Even something as simple as *Mario Paint* can be a valuable learning experience.

otherwise known as the creators of the Flash cartoon site HomestarRunner.com. Derived from a parody children's book that Mike Chapman and Craig Zobel wrote, the HomestarRunner cartoons and games were initially a way for the Chapman brothers to practice their Flash animation skills. Before that, they had even experimented with animation in *Mario Paint* on the Super Nintendo system, using some of their book characters.

Around 2000, they set up a site on Yahoo! to post their cartoons. The campy youth culture appeal of their characters drew so many visitors that not only does the site now have its own hosting, but millions of people visit the site on a regular basis. It's also not uncommon to see Trogdor T-shirts in the streets or fans toting Strong Bad Email DVDs (Tragdor and Strong Bad are characters in the HomestarRunner series of cartoons). But watching these cartoons isn't like watching TV because these cartoons are in Flash. And Flash allows Matt and Mike to hide "Easter eggs" (hidden extras) within the cartoons, as well as create mini-games to go with them. Some of the cartoons are interactive. Many of the games and cartoons parody elements of 1980s pop culture, like their fictitious video game company Videolectrix.

The site includes no advertising, but the sales from merchandise alone support Mike and Matt, as well as the site. Initially, HomestarRunner was a side job, but Mike and Matt's parents encouraged them to turn it into a full-time business. With help from their parents on the business aspects of it, they have full creative control over their work. Despite the high

number of characters they animate, Matt does the majority of the voices.

Mike and Matt didn't set out to be famous. In fact, Matt went to school for film, and Mike went to school for photography. But they pursued their interest in Flash animation and games, and eventually it became their livelihood. According to Matt, they don't have many out-side projects, but they try to incorporate on their site the skills they learned in school. Because the development of their site requires a number of different skills—pro-gramming, graphic art and design, animation, voice work, and project management (the ability to supervise workers and their tasks and get a project done on time and within budget)—Mike and Matt have created some-thing that shows off their abilities in a way that no résumé ever could.

These days, if you start a small gaming company, it can require a lot of time and effort to get noticed since advertising can cost a lot of money. Patience is a virtue. Not everybody becomes famous right off the bat, but there are plenty of opportunities to get noticed if you've made a good product. Sometimes the addictive nature of a game can help it get a lot of attention. Here are a couple of examples.

## A Diamond in the Rough—*Bejeweled*

In 2000, budding game company PopCap Games coded a simple puzzle game called *Bejeweled* that involved swap-ping two jewels around at a time to create rows or columns of three jewels of the same type. They intended to license it to Web portals and make money through ads

This *Bejeweled* page can be accessed directly (Bejewled.com) or via PopCap Games (PopCap.com). It offers a free Flash version that can be played from the site and a downloadable full version that must be paid for.

alongside the game. But coming on the heels of the dot-com bubble burst at the turn of the twenty-first century, that goal seemed less and less realistic. Instead, they decided to offer a free Flash version of the game, while simultaneously advertising a deluxe version that could be purchased separately (this is known as a "shareware" business model).

The strategy was unbelievably successful. Six years later, the game has been ported to nearly every platform available (mobile, console, etc.) and has sold approximately ten million units since 2001. Why? The first reason is that it is delightfully addictive. Second, not everybody has time to play first-person shooters or real-time strategy

## Alien Hominid

Don't assume that popular Flash games can catch on only through the Internet. In his spare time, the creator of Newgrounds.com, Tom Fulp, made a Flash game called *Alien Hominid* about a lovable alien being chased by FBI agents. It was originally uploaded to Newgrounds.com in 2002. *Alien Hominid* became so popular that a coworker at the game development house Fulp was working for asked him to start a new company with him and design a version of the game for consoles. Since its initial upload to the site, *Alien Hominid* has gotten more than six million downloads and is now available for the Xbox.

games, and some people just want something to do while they're riding the bus or sitting at their computer and taking a little break from work.

*Bejeweled* has seen many clones (*Zookeeper*, for the Nintendo DS, a handheld console, is similar) and has pioneered a market of games for the casual user. In 2005, 44 percent of frequent game players played games online, and 52 percent of games played online were puzzle, board, game show, trivia, or card games. *Bejeweled* has become the first puzzle game to be inducted into the Computer Gaming World's Hall of Fame since *Tetris*, in 1988.

*Bejeweled* is coded in Flash and is not very complex. Its graphics are attractive, but they are not astounding like those of *Halo* or *Final Fantasy*. The inspiration for *Bejeweled* (originally titled *Diamond Mine*) came from a simple, clunky JavaScript game using blocks that the developers discovered on the Internet one day. Realizing they could do better, they reinvented it using jewels and, in a matter of days, had a finished product they could show to portal sites. This is an example of how sometimes all it takes is simple, clever gameplay to make a game sell.

## BattleGoat Studios

Dave Thompson, George Geczy, and Chris Latour had been running a retail computer software store for fifteen years when they decided they needed a change. Having become familiar with the selection of PC games that were available, they decided that there was a niche they could fill—intelligent strategy games. None of them had gone to school for game design, but Geczy had coded a game called *Supreme Ruler* for the TRS-80 computer in 1982, while still in high school. This experience is what led him into software distribution in the first place.

In order to focus on the strategy game genre, Thompson, Geczy, and Latour sold their store and decided to resurrect *Supreme Ruler* as a strategy game. In an interview with the author, Thompson noted, "It was the type of game that we ourselves enjoyed playing, and there weren't many titles being developed in that genre." *Supreme Ruler 2010* is now a PC game that uses realistic military units, real-world map data (based on NASA satellite imagery), and accurate information about world resources and politics to create a strategy game that puts the player in control of the world's economic powers. It is as much a strategy simulation as a video game.

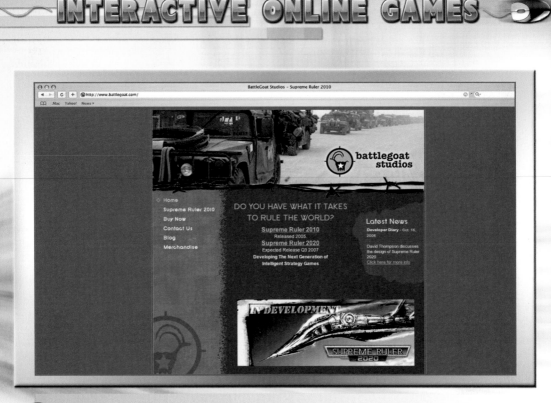

BattleGoat Studios promotes its upcoming and much anticipated game, *Supreme Ruler 2010*, on its Web site (BattleGoat.com).

Thompson, Geczy, and Latour initially used a publisher to market and distribute their game but eventually opted to do this themselves. Online distribution sites such as Zstorm and Digital River helped get their game to players. The game has enjoyed a surprising amount of success and has sold between 10,000 and 15,000 copies to date. This is a significant achievement, given the company's small size, limited distribution, the strength of the competition within the console market, and the fact that this was the very first game BattleGoat Studios produced.

Despite this success, Thompson, Geczy, and Latour's company remains small, employing only four people plus interns and contract workers. They intend

George Geczy, one of the founders of BattleGoat Studios, has proven that your hobbies and passion really can be your livelihood and can be put to very good use.

to keep it this way. A small company allows every employee to get involved in a variety of tasks, at every level of development. This helps both to avoid tedium and encourage problem solving. As Thompson says, "Regardless of what perceptions are out there, game development is a job. And like any job, it can get repetitive and frustrating. In a small development studio, we all wear many different hats, and if we get stuck on one task, we can switch hats and work on something else."

Like at many other game development companies, the employees of BattleGoat Studios familiarize themselves with each other's jobs. This familiarity and comfort level comes in handy when communicating about various tasks associated with a project and solving any problems that

*Supreme Ruler 2010*, despite a small budget and limited resources for distribution, won the award for Best PC Game from the Canadian Awards for the Electronic and Animated Arts.

may crop up. Every part of the process requires teamwork, and the team members have to understand each other's work and the time and effort involved. Being a small company means it's easier to come to a consensus, but it can be difficult when there's a lot of work involved. "Obviously there are some downsides to being a smaller developer," Thompson observes. "At crunch time there are only so many people around to get a job done, but we all feel that the benefits far outweigh the problems."

Designing games at a small company is not the most profitable job, but the BattleGoat designers are doing what they love. After all, making video games isn't necessarily a nine-to-five job. It requires long, often irregular hours and dedication. The people who are drawn to game programming and development do it because they have a serious drive to make games. They do whatever they can to make the sort of game that they want to see on the market, the sort of game that they want to play themselves.

Thompson illustrates this point and explains in the simplest terms how he and his partners pulled off something very difficult: "After fifteen years in retail, we were in need of a career change, so we decided to sell our business and try something different that we thought we would enjoy." The founders of BattleGoat Studios are living proof that following your passions and working on digital projects can in fact become your livelihood, and that it is never too late to put them to good use.

BattleGoat Studio's *Supreme Ruler 2010* has gotten a lot of attention as an "educational game" by sites like Artificial Wisdom. It has also won the award for Best PC Game from the Canadian Awards for the Electronic and Animated Arts.

Viewing an online computer game like *Supreme Ruler 2010* as educational is not such a stretch. A recent report by the MacArthur Foundation entitled *Confronting the Challenges of Participatory Culture: Media Education for the 21st Century* has concluded that games of all sorts, including video and computer games, can be learning experiences and opportunities to develop valuable skills. Things like attention and focus, and sustained effort are encouraged and required of game players. As the report says:

> The effort allows the person to master skills, collect materials, or put things in their proper place in anticipation of a payoff down the line. The key is that this activity is deeply motivated. The individual is willing to go through the grind because there is a goal or purpose that matters to the person. When that happens, individuals are engaged, whether that be the engagement in professional lives or the learning process or the engagement that some find through playing games. For the current generation, games may represent the best way of tapping that sense of engagement with learning.

So your interest in gaming, both as a player and a content creator, is not only providing you with marketable skills, it may also allow you to to help other young people learn and develop their own talents and abilities.

# CHAPTER THREE

# GAINING TOOLS, CREATING GAMES, AND SHOWING YOUR WORK

Teens today are surrounded by digital media—iPods, cell phones, video games, and all of the social interaction that comes with the online universe. You probably use instant messaging or VOIP (voice over Internet protocol) as much as the phone to talk to your friends, or YouTube as much as television for entertainment. You may have tried podcasting, and you might own an MP3 player (such as an iPod). You've probably been familiar with some form of digital or electronic media for a significant portion of your life, so your frame of reference will be drastically different from those of people older than you. You are less likely to be fazed or confused by emerging technologies, and mor

Rapid advances in technology have resulted in new products like video cel phones. These in turn have increased the platforms available for game des and players.

Video games are so popular that it's not uncommon to see people camped out-side of a store the night before a major game or console first hits the shelves, much like these devoted fans lined up to buy the PlayStation 3 in November 2006.

likely than people of your parents' generation to learn quickly how to use them.

## The Gamer Profile

It's no secret that video games in particular are a popular form of entertainment for youth, regardless of gender. BIGresearch did a study (commissioned by the National Retail Federation) of the top ten toys parents planned on buying their children for the 2006–2007 holiday season. For the boys, the top ten list included PlayStation 3, video games, Nintendo DS, and Xbox 360. For the girls, the top ten included iPod/MP3 players, Nintendo DS, and PlayStation 3.

According to the ESA, of the video games sold in 2005, 67.2 percent were action, sports, racing, or shooter games. The top-selling console game last year (by units sold) was *Madden NFL '06*. Other games among the top twenty best sellers, spanning a number of different genres, included *Star Wars Battlefront II*, *Lego Star Wars*, *Need for Speed: Most Wanted*, *SOCOM 3: US Navy SEALs*, *Grand Theft Auto: San Andreas*, and *God of War*. The top-selling computer game last year was *World of Warcraft*. Other games in the top twenty included *Sims 2*, *RollerCoaster Tycoon 3*, *Halo*, *Civilization IV*, and *MS Flight Simulator 2004: Century of Flight*.

But what is becoming more and more apparent to game makers and marketers is that gamers don't just game. They actually lead very busy, eclectic lives. According to the ESA's survey, "Gamers devote more than triple the amount of time spent playing games each week to exercising or playing sports, volunteering in the community, religious activities, creative endeavors, cultural activities, and reading." Gamers spend an average of 23.4 hours per week on those sorts of activities but only an average of 6.8 hours per week playing video games. In fact, 93 percent of gamers surveyed said that they read books or newspapers on a regular basis. Last year, 31 percent of gamers were under the age of eighteen (that's almost a third), and 80 percent of gamer parents said they play video games with their children.

## Developing Knowledge and Skills to Match Your Interests

Where your digital skills can take you depends entirely on the types of games and the parts of games that interest you the most. Do you like to draw? Do you like to write stories? Are you interested in how a game works?

There are many simple tools you can use to help you explore your digital skill, like 3-D modeling programs.

Whatever your particular game-based interest, there are a number of digital skills that can be developed immediately to help you gain hands-on experience and eventually find employment in the video game industry.

If you play MMORPGs or real-time strategy games, you might be interested in designing a level or changing some of the art in a game to better suit your own tastes. If you have an image editor like Adobe Photoshop, you might want to experiment with creating textures or manipulating photographs. If you like to write stories, maybe you'd like to write some dialogue to go with a game module. Or, if you play an instrument, you could try arranging a simple musical score as a game's soundtrack.

If you want to learn about basic game mechanics, you could play board games in addition to video games. There are many different types of board games (not just *Clue* or *Monopoly*) with many different styles of game-play. Many of them involve multiplayer strategy or role-playing very similar to that found in some video games (for instance, the video game *Supreme Ruler* is very similar to the board game *Diplomacy*). Consider the layout of a board game like *Settlers of Catan* and how you would adapt and improve it for use as a video game. Keep in mind that many video game designers started out by designing board games.

Not everybody can make Flash cartoons that will gain so much attention so quickly like those of Homestarrunner.com. But if you're creative enough, it's not hard to show off your best skills in the digital world. Much like Matt Chapman and Craig Zobel used *Mario Paint* as a starting point, you can find many cheap or free tools to experiment with.

If you already own a lot of games (this particularly applies to PC games), check to see if any of them come with editors or tool kits or can be downloaded off of the Internet. Some game companies, like Linden Lab (creators of *Second Life*) or Bioware (creators of *Neverwinter Nights*), encourage creativity in their community of players. Last January, Bioware held a writing contest that encouraged players to show off their dialogue-writing skills by creating a *Neverwinter Nights* module. One of the prizes was consideration for employment at the company. Bioware already offered many tools for creating custom *Neverwinter Nights* modules, so now they were merely

Everyone plays board games (even American troops serving in Afghanistan), and they're a booming business. Check out your local game or hobby shop and try as many as you can to get a feel for various types of game mechanics.

asking for playable samples, with a lot of dialogue. Bioware needed to draw on writing talent, so they appealed to their fan community to meet their needs.

 Editors allow you to easily change certain aspects of the game (the layout of a level or area, textures, sounds) or even design your own module or "mod"—a short, original, self-contained version of the game. In *Second Life*, you can design textures in Photoshop and import them directly into the game. BFBuilder, the editor for *Star Wars Battlefront*, lets you create your own units, maps, weapons, and even vehicles. It even works with programs like Softimage XSI.

Don't be afraid to try a simple 3-D modeling or animation program like Bryce 3D or 3DCanvas. Or, if you're even more ambitious, you might want to experiment with trial versions (or full versions, if you've got the money) of some of the programs the professionals use, such as Maya or 3D Studio Max. Macromedia Flash or Macromedia Director are incredibly useful tools for both practicing animation and experimenting with making interactive games. Adobe Photoshop is useful for creating textures by trying different filters on a picture you've drawn or taken. These programs might appear daunting at first, but there are lots of online tutorials and books at your local library for a variety of levels of expertise.

If you're interested in programming, choose a simple beginner language like HTML or Visual Basic to get a feel for how programming languages work and what sort of syntax they use. As for sound, a lot of electronic keyboards these days can be hooked up to a computer, and there are programs that let you simulate piano notes on your computer keyboard. There are many programs that allow you to assemble music or manipulate recorded sound effects.

## Machinima

You can do lots of creative things with video games, but did you know that some people even use them to make short films? The term that's used for this process is "machinima." Because video games as a medium are so flexible, they are an ideal way to make a short film even if you don't have the typical resources for making one. People will record in-game animation and edit it together with voice recordings to make a film. Games that have a lot of options for customization and gameplay work well, such as *World of Warcraft*, *The Sims 2*, or *The Movies*.

*Red vs. Blue*, by Rooster Teeth Productions, is probably one of the best-known examples of machinima. It takes place in Halo's Blood Gulch and chronicles the civil war between two futuristic fighting forces. The series has been so popular, in fact, that it is now in its fifth season and has even been released on DVD.

Another example of machinima, *This Spartan Life*, takes the video-game-as-short-film genre a step further by being an in-game talk show, featuring interviews with actual industry professionals and digital gurus in real time, over Xbox Live. The guests explore *Halo 2* with the hosts, while answering questions via voice chat.

This genre of film has become so popular that a yearly festival is now held, called the Machinima Festival. It is sponsored by some major players in the game industry, such as Nvidia and Linden Lab. For more information, check out http://festival.machinima.org.

## Showing and Sharing Your Work

If you enjoy making mods (or need some help doing so), join a mod community online to trade notes and get feedback. Some companies, like Bioware or LucasArts, provide hosting space for players to upload their mods so that other people can try them. The more you learn about how a particular game is put together or modified and participate actively (and constructively) in a fan community, the more you might stay informed about opportunities like beta testing. When a video game company is releasing a new product, it might first recruit some fans who are familiar with its other games to test an early, or "beta," version of a new product.

Aside from these communities, if you still want someplace to strut your stuff, you can upload pictures (or screenshots), music, and simple animations to sites that share them. There are many different types of modding sites. For example, on Newgrounds.com, you can upload Flash games or animation of any possible variety, whereas Ourmedia.org is considered a more professional-oriented site that hosts sound, images, and video. DeviantART is a close-knit community of visual artists and writers, many of whom are interested in Japanese anime- and manga-inspired drawing styles.

If you like to write stories, game reviews, or in-game news, it might be useful to maintain a blog or join a game development message board that has a writing section. You can pitch reviews to sites like Gamasutra or AdventureGamer.com. Video game stories are different from traditional media because they're nonlinear and

Newgrounds.com is a Web site that features a community of Flash animation and game developers. You can upload your work and get instant feedback. You can also use it to get a better idea of what's currently popular among game enthusiasts.

interactive—there can be multiple ways for the game's narrative to play out and resolve itself, depending on the player's skill, creativity, and choices. But you can still learn a lot from the plot structure and dialogue found in films and literature. Check out some books on cinematography, or pay attention to the directors' and screenwriters' commentaries on DVDs. For some theories on the most basic, classic, and enduring story archetypes, the often-recommended book is *The Hero with a Thousand Faces* by Joseph Campbell. There are also books on how to write for the interactive medium, like Chris Crawford's *Chris Crawford on Interactive Storytelling*.

One thing to keep in mind when uploading your work anywhere is what sort of permission you're giving to a site to use your work. For instance, most upload forms should have a "Terms of Use" agreement or something similar. Read these carefully. When you check the "I agree" box, you might be giving a site the right to unlimited use of your work without being compensated financially. You should decide ahead of time what you are comfortable with and stick to it. Newgrounds, for instance, allows all ownership rights to stay with the creator but reserves the nonexclusive right to show it on its site. EbaumsWorld.com, on the other hand, reserves an exclusive right to use the uploaded work and the creator's name/biography however it sees fit for three years and reserves a nonexclusive right after that.

As an alternative, when you post your work to your own Web site or blog, you can also apply what's called a Creative Commons license. This is a type of online certificate that specifies what viewers of your content are allowed to do with it if they want to redistribute it and show it to other people, while still giving you credit. For instance, you might have an animation or video posted in your blog. You can specify whether or not others can use it commercially (in a way that makes them money), whether they are allowed to modify it (like adding music or a watermark), and where the Creative Commons license applies (in your own country or all over the world). On CreativeCommons.org, you can choose your options, and the site will generate code that you can paste alongside your work. It can also provide you with a selection of Web sites like Flickr or DeviantART to post

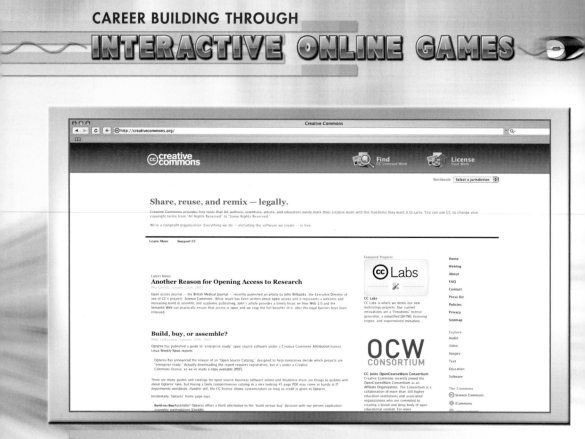

CreativeCommons.org allows you to generate a "license" for your content when sharing it on a Web site or blog.

the license to directly. A lot of videos and small games can become "viral" on the Internet, meaning people share them with their friends and upload them to other sites. A Creative Commons license will let people know how (and if) they can do that.

Also keep in mind that it's best not to share your phone number or address openly in your profile. Online exposure is a great way to get your work seen, but make sure that your name is attached only to works with content you feel comfortable sharing with prospective employers or teachers. You could even try Googling your own name periodically and see what results you get. Make sure there's nothing embarrassing!

Regardless of how you do it, there are plenty of online communities out there with which to share your work and get feedback. Experiment and look for other people who are working at the same level as you. And remember that there is always a variety of literature available both online and at your local library to help you figure out how best to get your work out there and available to as many people as possible.

# CHAPTER FOUR

# EDUCATION, ON-THE-JOB TRAINING, AND WORK EXPERIENCE

Turning an interest in video games into a career is a multistep process. First, you should decide which types of video games you enjoy the most and try to learn as much as you can about how they work. Then identify the aspect of gaming in which you are most interested (art, programming, sound) and experiment with the various tools available. Do some small projects and share them online to get some feedback. All of this activity and hands-on experience will allow you to create pieces that showcase your best talents. These pieces should then be gathered together in a portfolio. If you're considering a college degree in art, design, programming, or computer engineering, a portfolio will be your best bet

Graphic designers work with both digital and traditional media. In other words, you must be as good at drawing and sketching as you are at using graphic design software.

for showing how committed you are to learning about your category of interest.

## Laying the Educational Groundwork

**QUICK TIP** Plan your high school courses according to the major you hope to pursue in college. For programming, you'll need to take lots of math, like geometry, trigonometry, calculus, and algebra. Physics would also be useful. Take any programming courses your high school or local community college offers. Regardless of the programming language being taught, it will still provide useful experience. Animators study movement, so taking dance or drama might be a good complement to any art courses that you're taking. You'll need grounding in traditional art and drawing if you're considering becoming a concept artist. Learn as much about the basic parts of your interests as possible ahead of time, in high school, so you don't have to pay to learn the same information in college and can begin to gain specialized, higher-level knowledge that much sooner.

There are different types of post-secondary (post–high school) education to choose from. There are regular universities and colleges that offer courses in art, sound, and programming. Some of them, like the University of Southern California (USC), offer programs in game design. In the case of USC, it also offers a graduate program that is funded in part by a multimillion-dollar grant from Electronic Arts (EA; a leading video game maker) and offers internships.

Traditional four-year colleges and universities usually offer general education courses that aren't related to

College will provide you with essential professional skills and specialized knowledge, increasing your chances for creating a viable and successful career in your area of interest.

your field of interest. You will be required to take a wide variety of courses outside your major. Other schools are more specialized and narrowly focused. They allow you to become fully immersed in your specialty. Art schools like the Academy of Art University in San Francisco, California, now offer programs specifically for art in video games. They feature actual industry tools, gaming professionals, and game projects, but also offer foundation art courses in drawing, painting, metal, and other mediums. And there are also schools that are devoted only to video games, like DigiPen in Redmond, Washington, or Full Sail in Winter Park, Florida, where students go through the full process of creating a video game at least once, in addition to learning the subject matter.

## On-the-Job Experience

During the summer, you can seek game-related jobs like beta testing or work as an intern at one of the big video game companies. Be willing to take on nonpaying opportunities if they're the only ones available. The hands-on experience and industry contacts you can gain are invaluable and may result in a paying job in the future.

Do some research on the companies you like, and find out which ones offer internships. Some of the major companies, like Electronic Arts or Sony, offer them, but there are also smaller companies like BattleGoat Studios that use interns on a regular basis. Some companies will have a separate Web site for internship information, while others will just list the internship opportunities on their jobs page.

Testing jobs can often be found in the employment listings of various video game companies, but to see them all in one place, you can visit sites like Gamasutra.com or GameDev.net. Both have a jobs section listed by category. You may not have enough experience to get a testing job that pays, but there are always beta tests going on for games in development, so stay informed about your favorite company or visit a site like GamesTester.com to get information about current or upcoming beta tests. DigiPen offers summer workshops for middle school, high school, and college students looking to learn some basic skills in video game programming, art,

and sound. If your responses during a beta test are detailed, thoughtful, and insightful enough, they can speak volumes to a prospective employer about your gaming abilities and your potential value to the industry in general and their company in particular.

## Showcasing Your Work for Potential Employers

Before you even begin applying to college, you can showcase your work all in one place, by creating a portfolio Web site. Not only will you have a self-contained link to give to teachers and employers, but it's also a good chance to practice your skills in design, coding, or writing, since building a Web site often requires all three. It doesn't have to be complex or fancy. It should be clean and professional looking, with easy navigation. Keep it clear of too much personal material, like online diaries or photo albums. Because it's the Web, you can make a résumé in HTML that hyperlinks to examples of your work (hyperlinking can also be done in MS Word).

Domain names are relatively cheap and can easily be registered. But keep in mind that domain names don't always come with hosting space to store your pages and images, so make sure that you don't have a Web site with large video and picture files. In order to maximize your storage space, try to optimize your images for the Web as well as store audio and video in compressed formats such as MP3 or MPEG, or hosted on a separate site. Doteasy will give you a small amount of hosting space when you register a domain, and sites like YouTube and Photobucket are good for hosting media, as they have unlimited space and bandwidth.

A résumé and portfolio are essential for every college and employment interview. They show who you are, what you can do, and how committed you are to a professional attitude and appearance.

In terms of packaging your work to be able to show to people offline, interactive pieces can be burned to a CD. Make sure files are in a typical format that most computers can read, like MS Word, Flash, MPEG, and MP3, and they are complete and relatively self-contained. Always bring to an interview a hard-copy version of noninteractive elements of your portfolio, like your résumé, articles, and pictures/screenshots. Put all of these elements together in a binder or folder with transparency sheets so that you don't lose anything.

In the interview, make sure you are dressed professionally. In the game industry, business-casual is often acceptable, but when interviewing with a college, dress as

professionally as possible. It never hurts to wear a suit, or at least a jacket and tie. Jeans, sneakers, and T-shirts are frowned upon in interviews, even within the video game industry. This is a career, and you should treat the company, the interviewer, and the potential job with the respect they deserve. In addition to dressing nicely, show this respect by doing research on the company and demonstrating during the interview that you've learned some things about what the company does, its products, its history, and its performance in the marketplace. This will both impress and flatter your potential employers.

**GameDev.net:** Founded in 1999, GameDev.net is one of the most comprehensive online communities to cater directly to aspiring game developers. It was made for, and by, its members. GameDev.net includes a message board that covers all possible categories related to game development, where you can register and post for free, ask questions and seek the advice of other members, and collaborate with your fellow board members. You can log on to the chat room and check out the listings for in-person get-togethers in your area.

Also check out the tutorials, product reviews, member-written columns, and a weekly newsletter to keep you up to date on the latest news. There is a section called "For Beginners" that tackles frequently asked questions. GameDev.net is also a good place to find listings for the latest jobs and contests available in the industry.

Even more important, GameDev offers the "GDnet Showcase," where members can upload and try out playable finished projects or works in progress created by fellow GameDev members. This is a good way for game developers of all skill and experience levels to get feedback on their projects.

## Résumé

You may already be familiar with how to lay out a résumé, but if you're composing it with the game industry or a digital career in mind, there are a few special considerations to keep in mind.

Be sure to list all of your computer- and programming-specific skills—what software packages or programs you're familiar with, scripting languages, tool sets, and whatever else you have experience with that is relevant. Be prepared to answer questions about these skills and programs when you show the résumé to people. Think of how you would describe those skills in person, and never list something that you are not truly familiar or experienced with. List applicable courses or internships that you've completed and any relevant work experience that you have gained.

Don't forget to list your contributions for each gaming project you've been involved in, and always include good references—people who can speak knowledgeably and favorably about your skills, work habits, and personal character. This way, possible employers won't be contacting people who have an unfavorable opinion of you. Always notify your references to let them know you are using them as references so they will not be caught off guard and unprepared when a call comes in.

Keep a list of companies you're interested in and check their job boards regularly for postings that may apply to you. Familiarize yourself with important people in those companies, follow their careers, and look for legitimate opportunities to meet or correspond with them.

# CHAPTER FIVE

# GAMING CAREERS AND NETWORKING

There are many different parts to a video game. If you consider *Bungie's Halo* alone, you realize that there are different people assigned to the designing of different parts of the game—someone to design the green grass textures on the ground, someone to code how the jeep moves when it gets flipped over, someone to orchestrate the sounds of crickets chirping in the background, and so on.

## Designing, Programming, and Other Game-Related Careers

Game designers have most of the creative control over a game and put together the design document, which is a

A computer animation designer works on a project at Zhongnan Animation studios in Hangzhou, China.

plan for the whole game—the characters, the story, the setting, the gameplay. Artists first draw concept sketches to flesh out what the characters or objects look like and then model them in 3-D or animate them. Artists also create textures and determine how things will look under different levels of light. Sound designers create the sound effects for various activities in the game as well as design music that moves along as the story (or game action) moves along.

Programmers create or tweak the "engine" of the game, which powers how the game is controlled and how things in the game move or work. *Unreal Tournament*, for instance, has an engine that is used by students studying game development, since adapting it and using it for a project can be valuable in learning game programming without starting from scratch. Numerous documentation on using the *Unreal* engine exists, including a site at http://udn.epicgames.com. If you plan on designing computer software in the future, game programming might be a good portfolio piece. Likewise, you could also use character designs or art for a game as part of an art portfolio.

Not all careers related to video games deal directly with designing them. There are also jobs in computer game marketing, business, accounting, and journalism, to name a few. Journalists and writers who specifically have an interest in video games can pitch articles and reviews to sites like Gamasutra.com or magazines like *Game Developer*. Since the video game industry can be a lightning rod for controversy and speculation (particularly concerning violent and sexual content), there is

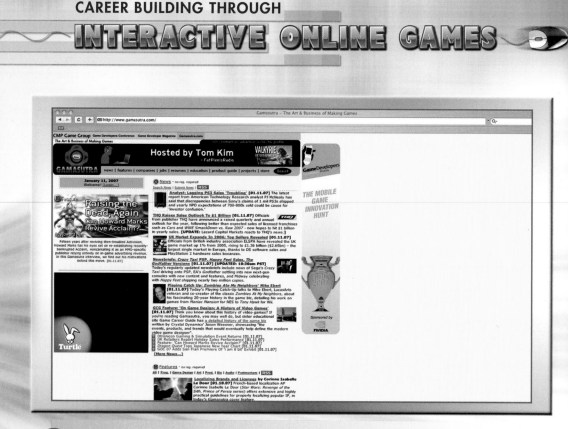

Gamasutra.com collects and posts articles, reviews, and reports from game journalists who keep a close watch on emerging industry trends.

always a need for writers who are passionate about video games and who can think and write critically about what's happening in the industry and what effect certain games are having on their users and on society at large.

## Small Projects and Networking

Employers and colleges aren't just looking for "hard skills" like programming languages or concept drawing. They're also looking for "soft skills"—leadership, team-work, organization, self-discipline, and the ability to work to a deadline. They're not just looking for past jobs or school grades but also smaller projects that you take your own initiative on.

## Game Developers Conference

Started in 1987 by industry guru Chris Crawford, the Game Developers Conference caters to game companies and professionals by hosting awards, roundtable discussions, and previews of upcoming games and console technology. It is a prime place to network with potential employers and meet future colleagues in a relaxed, comfortable environment. GDC offers an accurate reflection of where the industry is heading. Over the past few years, it has added subconferences like GDC Mobile and the Serious Games Summit to keep pace with the latest technological developments and gaming trends.

The GDC also includes the Independent Games Festival, which offers thousands of dollars in awards to the most innovative independent game developers. The IGF is split into three categories: the main competition, the mod competition, and the student showcase. Even young, amateur game developers have a chance to make an impression at this festival competition and win some money at the same time.

The other major component of the GDC is the Game Connection, where developers can connect with buyers, publishers, and distributors, and show a little bit of what they have to offer. Overall, it is the most important industry event of the year. It takes place in California (usually in San Francisco or San Jose), but if you can't attend, sites like Gamasutra generally offer detailed coverage of the event, in some cases including podcasts and streaming video.

Teamwork and the ability to take direction are important in the video game industry.

There are small projects that you can do by yourself, like short animations, scripts, and edited levels and mods. But it's also worthwhile to meet other people at the same level as you—but with different skill sets— and team up for something bigger and more ambitious. If you don't already have friends or acquaintances who could partner with you, the best way to find fellow game developers is to network. You can do this online by joining a Web community like GameDev.net or social networking sites like Friendster or MySpace, or you can trying meeting people in person. Look for video game–related trade shows, conventions, or social events in your area.

Joining a club like this after-school computer gaming club at Travis High School in Austin, Texas, not only helps you meet others with the same interests, but it can also broaden your knowledge of different types of video games.

You can also visit IGDA.org (International Game Developers Association) and find the closest chapter to you and where and when they meet. Most chapters hold monthly social nights or other events for members to get together. Dress neatly and semicasually and be prepared to talk to both industry professionals and ambitious students about what you know and what you'd like to learn. Contacts that you make now, even with people at the same level as you, may come in handy in the future. Remember that how you present yourself will go a long way toward making a good impression. Don't be rude or obnoxious. Someone important could remember you for the wrong reasons. When you do have an opinion to offer, offer it in a

Always try to keep up on the latest trends in the video game industry, like the "casual games" genre being practiced in this photo.

constructive and intelligent manner. Make people remember you for your thoughtfulness, creativity, good manners, knowledge, and intelligence.

## A Passion for Gaming

The bottom line is that people who work in the industry are passionate about video games. Every employee in the industry has to know video games primarily through playing them, and he or she should love playing them almost all the time. If you really want to get an idea of what's out there, try playing different sorts of games, even ones you wouldn't normally play. Develop a sense of industry history, and play and become familiar with old games, like *Pac-Man* or *Space Invaders*. But most of all, play the kind you like, a lot. Every game that you play can be a learning experience. You'll learn what works, what doesn't, what is entertaining, what is challenging, and what is stimulating.

# GLOSSARY

**blog** A shortened version of "Web log," blogs began as a popular method of sharing a personal journal with a wide readership. They now encompass a variety of subjects and forms, such as politics or consumer electronics, but are generally first-person, instantly published content in a "journal" form.

**Blu-ray** A next-generation optical disc that uses a blue-violet laser to record, rewrite, and playback high- definition video and store large amounts of data.

**CD-ROM** A compact disc that contains data that can be read by a computer.

**download** To transfer data from a large computer to the memory of another device, usually a smaller computer.

**Flash** A program developed by the software company Adobe that allows users to add animation and interactivity to Web sites. Flash is commonly used to create animation, advertisements, and Web page components. It can also integrate video into Web pages.

**high-definition (HD) video** Video of a higher resolution than standard definition video, resulting in improved visual detail, sharpness, and clarity.

**interface** The ability for unrelated, independent systems, such as two or more computers, to communicate with each other.

**MMORPG (massively multiplayer online role-playing game)** These are online game "universes" that allow players to create and customize a character and play, in real time, through various scenarios/adventures with other players. Examples include *World of Warcraft*, *City of Heros*, *Everquest*, and *Anarchy Online*.

**mobile** Any electronic appliance, such as a cell phone or personal digital assistant (PDA), that uses wireless telephone networks.

**MP3** A digital audio encoding and compression format that greatly reduces the amount of data required to faithfully reproduce digitally recorded sounds, such as music and speech, when played back.

**online** Connected to, served by, or available through a computer or telecommunications system; something done while connected to a system.

**podcast** A digitally recorded audio file that is distributed over the Internet and can be played back by individuals using MP3 players or personal computers. The content of the podcast can be anything that can be stored in an audio file—radio shows, concerts, lectures, school lessons, public safety messages, audio tours, author readings, spoken words, poetry slams, roundtable discussions, etc. The same technology can be used with video files to create video podcasts, sometimes known as vidcasts or vodcasts.

**simulation** A system's imitation of another system's function or process. For example, if fed the proper data, a computer can simulate a region's likely

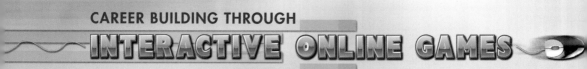
weather patterns, allowing for accurate weather
forecasting.

**software** The programs and procedures associated with
a computer system; computer programs.

**upload** To transfer data from one computer to a remote
computer, usually with the help of a modem.

# FOR MORE INFORMATION

Academy of Art University
Admissions Department
79 New Montgomery Street, 4th Floor
San Francisco, CA 94105-3410
(800) 544 -2787
Web site: http://www.academyart.edu

Academy of Interactive Arts
  and Sciences
23622 Calabasas Road, Suite 220
Calabasas, CA 91302
(818) 876-0826
Web site: http://www.interactive.org

CMP Game Group
Web site: http://www.cmpgame.com

Entertainment Software Association
575 7th Street NW, Suite 300
Washington, DC 20004
Web site: http://www.theesa.com

Independent Game Developers
  Association
Brighton Business Centre
95 Ditchling Road
Brighton, England BN1 4ST
Web site: http://www.tiga.org

International Game Developers
  Association
19 Mantua Road
Mt. Royal, NJ 08061
(856) 423-2990
Web site: http://www.igda.org

## Web Sites

Due to the changing nature of Internet links, Rosen
Publishing has developed an online list of Web sites
related to the subject of this book. This site is updated
regularly. Please use this link to access the list:

http://www.rosenlinks.com/dcb/cbig

# FOR FURTHER READING

Adams, Ernest. *Break into the Game Industry*. New York, NY: McGraw-Hill Osborne Media, 2003.

Ahearn, Luke, and Clayton E. Crooks. *Awesome Game Creation: No Programming Required*. Revere, MA: Charles River Media, 2002.

Darby, Jason. *Make Amazing Games in Minutes*. Revere, MA: Charles River Media, 2005.

Game Developer. *Fall 2006 Game Career Guide*. Manhasset, NY: CMP Technology, 2006.

Jenkins, Henry, et al. *Confronting the Challenges of Participatory Culture: Media Education for the 21st Century*. Chicago, IL: The MacArthur Foundation, 2006.

Pardew, Les, and Alpine Studios. *Game Design for Teens*. Boston, MA: Thomson Course Technology PTR, 2004.

Sethi, Maneesh. *Game Programming for Teens*. 2nd ed. Boston, MA: Thomson Course Technology PTR, 2005.

# BIBLIOGRAPHY

"Alien Hominid." AlienHominid.com. 2004. Retrieved November 2006 (http://www.alienhominid.com/ the_game/game.html).

"Bejeweled." Wikipedia. Retrieved November 2006 (http://en.wikipedia.org/wiki/Bejeweled).

"Creative Commons Licenses." Creative Commons. Retrieved November 2006 (http://creativecommons. org/about/licenses/meet-the-licenses).

Crowe, Samuel. "Applying for Your First Game Industry Job." GameCareerGuide.com. 2006. Retrieved January 2007 (http://www.gamecareerguide.com/ features/264/applying_for_your_first_game_.php).

Entertainment Software Association. *Essential Facts About the Computer and Video Game Industry.* Washington, DC: Entertainment Software Association, 2006.

Game Developer. *Fall 2006 Game Career Guide.* Manhasset, NY: CMP Technology, 2006.

"Homestar Runner." Wikipedia. Retrieved November 2006 (http://en.wikipedia.org/wiki/Homestarrunner).

Jenkins, Henry, et al. *Confronting the Challenges of Paricipatory Culture: Media Education for the 21st Century.* Chicago, IL: The MacArthur Foundation, 2006.

Lee, Raina. "Meet the Machinimakers: The 2006 Machinima Festival Report." Gamasutra.com. November 21, 2006. Retrieved January 2007 (http:// www.gamasutra.com/features/20061121/ lee_01.shtml).

McElroy, Justin. "Behind the Game Bejeweled."
    GameZebo. September 21, 2006. Retrieved
    November 2006 (http://www.gamezebo.com/
    2006/09/behind_the_game_bejeweled.html).
National Retail Federation. "Holiday Consumer
    Intentions and Actions Survey." BIGresearch.
    December 2006. Retrieved December 2006 (http://
    www.bigresearch.com/news/bignrf111606.htm).
Thompson, David. E-mail interview with author.
    November 21, 2006.

# INDEX

## W
*World of Warcraft* game, 7,
27, 32

## X
Xbox, 26, 32

## Y
Yahoo! search engine, 15
YouTube.com, 25, 42

## Z
Zstorm, 20

## About the Author

Meg Swaine is a writer living in southern Ontario, Canada. She specializes in topics related to the Web and interactivity. Swaine has a BA in creative writing from York University, as well as a diploma in online writing and information design from Centennial College (both in Toronto). She is currently addicted to the virtual world *Second Life* and carries a pink Nintendo DS with her on the bus.

## Photo Credits

Cover and title page video game controller, console Shutterstock.com; Cover and title page laptop © www. istockphoto.com/Lisa Thornberg; Cover and title page video game image, pp. 25, 28, 40, 46 © AFP/Getty Images; p. 4 © Manchester Daily Express/SSPL/The Image Works; p. 6 © SSPL/The Image Works; pp. 10, 11, 12, 26, 30 © Getty Images; p. 14 © Time Life Pictures/Getty Images; pp. 20, 21, 22 © BattleGoat Studios; p. 38 © age fotostock/SuperStock; p. 43 © www.istockphoto.com/Jilian Pond; p. 50 © Catherine Karnow/Corbis; p. 51 © Bob Daemmrich/The Image Works; p. 52 © AP/Wide World Photos.

Designer: Nelson Sa
Photo Researcher: Cindy Reiman